YOU CHOOSE
BOOKS™

HANSEL AND GRETEL

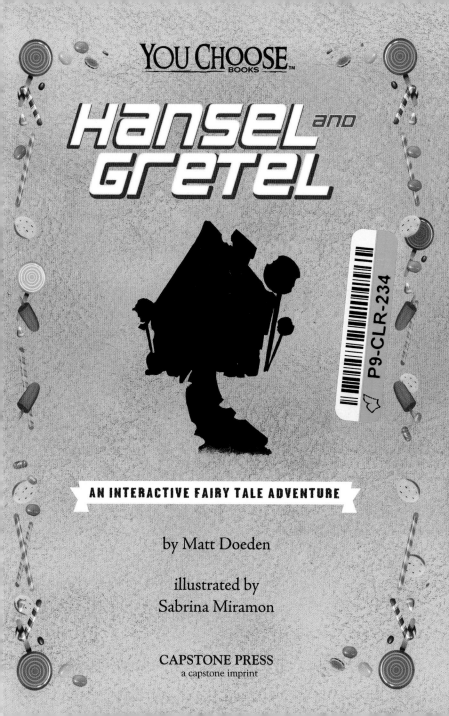

AN INTERACTIVE FAIRY TALE ADVENTURE

by Matt Doeden

illustrated by
Sabrina Miramon

CAPSTONE PRESS
a capstone imprint

P9-CLR-234

You Choose Books are published by Capstone Press,
1710 Roe Crest Drive, North Mankato, Minnesota 56003
www.mycapstone.com

Library of Congress Cataloging-in-Publication Data
Library of Congress Cataloging-in-Publication data is available on the Library of
Congress website.
978-1-5157-6944-6 (library binding)
978-1-5157-6952-1 (paperback)
978-1-5157-6955-2 (eBook PDF)

Editorial Credits
Michelle Hasselius, editor; Lori Bye, designer; Bob Lentz, art director;
Gene Bentdahl, production specialist

Image Credits
Shutterstock: solarbird, background

Printed and bound in the United States of America.
032018   000013

TABLE OF CONTENTS

YOU are about to enter a world filled with magic, mystery . . . and candy. A world where your wildest dreams are within reach. And isn't it good to grab for your dreams? Maybe not. At least not in these tales. Whether you're a witch, an explorer on an uncharted planet, or a kid lost in a virtual world, some treats might be too good to be true.

In this fairy tale, you control your fate. Chapter One sets the scene. Then you choose which path to read. Follow the directions at the bottom of the page as you read the stories. The decisions you make will change your outcome. After you finish one path, go back and read the others for new perspectives and more adventures.

TOO MUCH OF A GOOD THING?

Gingerbread, candy, cakes . . . everywhere you look, you're surrounded by them. You find yourself in a wild and fantastic world, and it seems to be filled with delicious treats. Your mouth is watering. All you have to do is reach out and grab them.

Of course it's not as simple as that. Nothing comes without a price. And the price may be steep for these tasty treats. Because for every move you make, *someone* is watching. *Someone* is waiting.

7

The fire in the oven is stoked. As you look around, you can't help but wonder what is next on today's menu. A little voice inside your head keeps warning: Maybe it's *you*.

You step forward and take a deep breath. The smell of sugar and flour fill the air. The time has come. It's time to make the choice that could alter the course of your life forever.

TO EXPERIENCE THE CLASSIC FAIRY TALE OF HANSEL
AND GRETEL FROM THE WITCH'S POINT OF VIEW, 9
TURN TO PAGE 11.

TO BLAST INTO SPACE WITH YOUR BROTHER
FOR A FUTURISTIC TWIST ON THE TALE,
TURN TO PAGE 47.

TO DIVE INTO THE DEPTHS OF A DARK AND DANGEROUS
VIRTUAL FAIRY-TALE WORLD,
TURN TO PAGE 77.

CHAPTER 2

STOP EATING MY HOUSE!

It's a lovely autumn evening. The sound of hooting owls wafts in through your open window as you add wood to your oven.

It's the perfect time to bake gingerbread, and you're going to need a lot of it. Ever since the kids from the nearby village discovered your house, it's been a constant battle to keep things standing. They break off pieces of the gingerbread walls. They run off with your candy-cane fence posts. They even eat the chocolate candies that you use to pave your walk. It makes you wonder if having a house made of candy is even worth the trouble.

"Honestly," you mutter to yourself as you sprinkle powdered sugar onto a slab of gingerbread. "I'm going to have to do something about this."

As much as you love children, you can't keep rebuilding. You tried posting a sign that read: PLEASE DON'T EAT MY HOUSE. But they ate the sign. In hindsight maybe you shouldn't have made it out of peanut brittle. You tried spreading a rumor that you were a witch, hoping the idea would scare them off. That didn't work either. Apparently kids are willing to risk a witch's wrath if there's enough candy on the line.

Your thoughts drift as you put the pan of gingerbread into the oven.

Ah, you think. *Nothing like baking to calm the nerves.*

Just then you hear it: Voices. They're small and quiet. It's a boy and a girl, and they're fairly young from the sound of them. You strain to hear them.

"What is this place?" asks the girl.

"Look, Gretel!" says the boy. "Candy. Everywhere you look, candy! It's like a dream!"

"I'm so hungry, Hansel," says the girl. "Can we eat some? Just a little bit?"

To your disappointment you hear a small *Snap!* They've broken off a piece of the house. Gretel squeals with delight as she munches away. What are you to do?

TO GIVE THE CHILDREN A GENTLE WARNING, TURN TO PAGE 14.

TO TRY TO SCARE THEM AWAY, TURN TO PAGE 17.

"Nibble, nibble, like a mouse," you call out. "Who is gnawing at my house?"

For a moment all you hear is silence. Then in a small and frightened voice, Hansel answers, "The wind."

You roll your eyes. They don't expect you to believe that, do they? But you've called out to them. That should be enough to send them on their way. You glance back at your oven. The smell of gingerbread is beginning to fill the house. You breathe it in deeply as your stomach growls.

Snap! comes the sound from outside. *Munch! Munch! Munch!*

"They're at it again?" you say to yourself.

You throw open the door and step out into the cool evening air, prepared to give the thieves an earful. The children cower in fear. They're dressed in rags, covered in dirt, and look painfully thin. The sight of them instantly melts your anger away. These poor children look like they're starving!

"Oh, you dear children," you say kneeling down and opening your arms. "Do come inside. I won't hurt you. Let's get you something to eat." The children come inside. You make them pancakes, which they devour.

"We haven't had more than bread for weeks," Gretel tells you. The little girl's huge grin brightens the whole room. You're so glad that you didn't chase these children away.

TURN THE PAGE.

The sun is getting low in the sky. The trees outside cast long shadows.

"Oh my, look at how late it's getting," you say. "I'm so sorry, your parents must be worried." Both children look down at the table. Gretel's grin is replaced by a frown.

"Our stepmother doesn't want us," Hansel says, his tone somber. "She made our father — the woodcutter — leave us in the woods. That's how we came to find your house."

The idea shocks you. Who would leave these precious children alone in the woods? It's unthinkable! You have to do something.

TO LET THE CHILDREN STAY WITH YOU,
TURN TO PAGE 20.

TO TAKE THEM HOME AND SPEAK WITH THEIR FATHER,
TURN TO PAGE 30.

You could have a chat with the children, but right now you just don't feel like it. Putting a good scare into them sounds like a lot more fun. Nobody seems frightened by the rumors you spread about being a witch. So maybe a little demonstration will help get the word out.

A broom and dust pan stand by the door. You use them to keep the front step clean and crumb free. You grab the broom, put on your scariest face, and charge out the front door with a wild shriek.

The looks on the children's faces almost make you burst out laughing. Their eyes grow wide, and their jaws drop. Both children are covered in dirt and gingerbread crumbs. Hansel steps back so quickly that he trips over Gretel's feet. They both go down in a heap of squirming arms and legs.

"I'll teach you a lesson for messing with
a witch," you shriek. "I'll eat you for supper!"
The children scramble to their feet and take
off running.

You run after them, waving your broom around and pretend that you're going to whack them with it. Of course you'd never do that. But *they* don't know that.

You chase the children around the woods until you have them cornered up against your front door. They have nowhere to go. As you move toward them, the children fling open your door and dash inside.

How dare they enter my home! you think. You follow behind them. The children back away toward your oven, cowering in fear.

TO CHASE THE CHILDREN OUT OF YOUR HOUSE, TURN TO PAGE 41.

TO STOP THE ACT AND TALK TO THEM, TURN TO PAGE 43.

"Don't you worry," you say to the children. "You can stay with me for a bit. I have more than enough food, and I could use some help around the house."

Hansel lets out a huge sigh of relief. Gretel squeals, jumps out of her chair, and wraps you up in the biggest hug her tiny arms can manage.

"Thank you, thank you!" she says. "We'll be so good. We're hard workers too."

You set up two small beds in the corner. Before bedtime Gretel asks for a story. "Father always tells us a bedtime story," she says. "Please?"

She asks so sweetly that you can't refuse. But you don't know many kids' stories. Instead, you tell them a story about a witch who eats children for dinner. It leaves both children wide-eyed and clutching their sheets.

"Now, now," you say with a laugh. But as you speak, a scratch in your throat makes you start to cough. It makes your laugh sound more like a cackle. "Don't be afraid of that silly old story," you reassure them, tucking them in. "Go to sleep. Tomorrow will be a big day."

Soon both children are snoring away. You love having them here, but you start wonder if you've have gotten in over your head. What do you know about taking care of children? You aren't even sure what to feed them. They can't eat candy all day.

Humming a soft tune, you grab a cookbook from your bookcase. It's a dusty old volume that your mother gave you years ago. You've never needed to use it until now. The title, *Cooking for Children*, is so faded that you can barely read it. The second word is almost worn away entirely.

You flip through the book. After a while you set it down on the bookcase and go to bed. In the morning you awaken to the clang and clatter of the children doing the dishes.

"Well how lovely," you tell them. "You don't have to do that."

"We want to," Hansel says. "You've done so much for us."

"What are we going to do today?" Gretel asks, her eyes wide and hopeful.

23

TO SPEND THE DAY BAKING,
TURN TO PAGE 24.

TO TAKE A WALK IN THE WOODS,
TURN TO PAGE 27.

"I think," you say while placing your hand on Gretel's back, "that today is a good day for baking." Gretel is so thin. You can see every rib in her body through her shirt. "I believe we need to fatten you up a bit."

You grab a towel and help dry the dishes. The three of you break into a song as you work. Gretel has a nice voice. Neither you nor Hansel could carry a tune to save your lives. You laugh at yourselves and enjoy each other's company.

"We're so lucky we found you," Hansel says.

"Oh I'm the lucky one," you insist. "I do so love spending time with you children. I didn't realize how lonely I was out here in this house by myself." You turn your head as a tear rolls down your face.

"Now let's do some baking," you say, gaining your composure. "Hansel, will you grab me the cookbook on that bookcase?"

As you lean over to add wood to the fire, Hansel steps over and picks up the book. He glances down at it as he starts back toward you. Then he freezes.

"What is it, young man?" you ask.

He looks terrified. "N-n-nothing." he stammers. "I, um, I just . . ."

You shrug. He's shy. Well you're determined to make the kids feel welcome. And the best way to do that is to let them help you. It's time for a baking lesson.

25

TURN THE PAGE.

"Gretel, will you come over here?" you ask. "I want to show you how hot the fire should be to bake. I have a recipe I've been wanting to try, but I need a couple of special ingredients to make it perfect."

"Don't move, Gretel!" Hansel shouts. "She's going to eat us!"

"What?" you gasp. "Where did you get that crazy idea?"

"Look," Hansel says, holding the cookbook. The title appears to be *Cooking Children*. Gretel backs away from you. She doesn't know what to believe.

TO TRY TO COMFORT GRETEL,
TURN TO PAGE 32.

TO GRAB THE BOOK FROM HANSEL,
TURN TO PAGE 34.

Gretel helps you pack a picnic lunch of gingerbread, jelly beans, and lollipops. Then the three of you venture out into the woods for a hike. You sing songs as you walk along the winding trails near your home. You spot birds, bear cubs, and even a few fairies along the way. The sun is shining, and a gentle breeze blows through the leaves. Life couldn't be better.

Hansel and Gretel are enjoying your picnic in a quiet meadow. In the distance you spot some fallen elm trees.

"Children, do you like mushrooms?" you ask.

Both kids scrunch up their noses. "Ewww," Gretel says.

Well *they* may not like mushrooms, but you love them. And elm trees have some of the best. "Enjoy your candy, children. I'll be right back."

The trees are a bit farther away than you guessed. By the time you reach them, you can't hear the children talking and laughing anymore.

"I'll make this a quick stop," you murmur. Just as you find a nice bunch of mushrooms, you hear a sound. *Thwack! Thwack! Thwack!*

It takes you a moment to realize what it is — it's the sound of an axe cutting into wood.

"The woodcutter," you whisper. It must be Hansel's and Gretel's father. Silently you creep through the woods toward the sound.

There he is! The woodcutter is a powerfully built man. His shoulders are broad and his arms are muscular. On each arm is a tattoo — a G on the right and an H on the left. He's chopping wood, splitting off huge sections with each swipe of his massive blade. His expression is distant and . . . sad.

29

TO TELL THE WOODCUTTER THAT HIS CHILDREN ARE OK,
TURN TO PAGE 36.

TO GET AWAY FROM HIM AS QUICKLY AS POSSIBLE,
TURN TO PAGE 39.

You stand up, take Gretel by the hand, and announce, "Come now, children. I'll take you home."

Hansel quickly eats a few final bites of his pancake. "We left a trail of bread crumbs so we could find our way home," he explains.

The woods grow darker as the three of you make your way. By the time you reach the woodcutter's little cottage, you have only the light of the moon to see by.

You approach the home. Smoke puffs out of the small chimney. Through an open window, you can hear people talking inside.

"It's much nicer without those children," says a woman's voice. "There's so much more food for us!"

Swallowing down your anger, you pound on the door. "Open up," you shout.

The door opens, and a woman stands before you. Her jaw drops. Behind her stands a tall, muscular man. Your anger makes you act out. You force your way inside, shoving the woman.

"It's the witch!" the woman cries. "She's come to kill us!" The man grabs his giant axe.

"No, no . . .," you try to explain, but it's too late. The woodcutter raises his axe. You know that he won't miss his mark.

THE END

TO FOLLOW ANOTHER PATH, TURN TO PAGE 9.

"Sweet girl," you say, reaching your arms out toward Gretel. "I just want to—"

Before you can finish, Hansel pushes you away from his sister. You stumble, almost falling over. You throw your arms out to steady yourself. But as you do, you accidentally hit Hansel. The boy lets out a muffled grunt and falls to the floor. Gretel screams. It's loud and shrill. You know what it means — Gretel thinks you're a witch.

You quickly turn your attention to Hansel. He's lying a few feet in front of the oven, which is growing hotter by the moment. That's not a safe place for him. You reach down to grab him under the shoulders and move him to safety. Just then Gretel's scream turns into a defiant yell. You turn and feel the impact of her little body against your own.

Gretel is small, but she packs a punch. The push sends you backward into the hot oven.

"This is what I get for trying to help the children who eat my house!" you think as you fall into the deadly fire. *"I'll never do that again!"*

33

And of course you never do.

THE END

TO FOLLOW ANOTHER PATH, TURN TO PAGE 9.

You step forward and snatch the book from Hansel's hands. He recoils in fear.

"You've got it all wrong," you explain, as both children slowly back away toward the door. "When I said I wanted to bake today, I didn't mean I wanted to bake *you!*"

The children stop retreating. They're listening.

"You're so thin. We need to fatten you up, see?" They start to back away again. "Look, look!" you fling the book open to a random recipe without looking. "See? It's not what you think. It's just a cookbook!"

Gretel screams, and you look down. The recipe you opened is for miniature ladyfingers.

"No, no! This is all a misunderstanding!" you insist, stepping toward the cowering children.

"Run!" Hansel shouts. He grabs Gretel by the wrist, and they bolt out of the door.

"Come back, children" you call running after them. "We were having such fun together!"

But they run deeper into the woods. Finally you stop, try to catch your breath, and put your hands on your hips. It's a long, slow walk back to your home, which suddenly seems lonely.

You never forget Hansel and Gretel. Every time you hear the *Snap!* of a child breaking off a piece of your home, you hope that they have returned to you. But they never do. Perhaps one day your candy home will lure in some other children in need of a friend. Perhaps you won't always be alone here in the woods.

THE END

TO FOLLOW ANOTHER PATH, TURN TO PAGE 9.

After a deep breath, you step out into the opening. "Hello," you call.

For a moment the woodcutter appears startled. "Well, hello," he says.

"You don't know me, but there's something you should see," you say cautiously. "Come with me."

You lead the woodcutter through the woods and back to the meadow where Hansel and Gretel are finishing their picnic. They look up as you emerge, their eyes growing wide.

Gretel springs to her feet. She rushes to her father and leaps into his arms. Hansel hesitates. After a few moments, he hugs his father as well. The strong man's face is covered in tears. Meanwhile Gretel is frantically trying to tell him about everything that happened.

" . . . and the walls are made of *gingerbread!*"
Gretel squeals. "And we ate and ate, and there was
a story about a witch, but it wasn't a real witch, and
we saw fairies, and . . . and . . ."

The woodcutter wipes his face dry and shakes your hand. "Thank you so much for keeping them safe. I'll never, ever leave them again. I've missed them so much."

The walk home is long and lonely. You're happy that your new friends got to go home. But you can't help feeling sad that they're not with you.

When you finally make it back home, the sun is beginning to set. You sigh as you see your house. Half of the east wall is missing. Little tooth marks are all over your candy-cane fence posts.

38

"Oh well," you sigh. "It's time to get back to my baking."

THE END

TO FOLLOW ANOTHER PATH, TURN TO PAGE 9.

"I won't lose them," you whisper to yourself.

You rush back to the meadow as quietly as you can. You can still hear the faint *Thwack! Thwack! Thwack!* Luckily the children don't seem to notice.

"Hurry along now," you tell them. "I smell a storm in the air. We must hurry back to the house!"

Hansel and Gretel follow your directions without any questions. Within a few minutes, you're headed back home — in the opposite direction from where you saw the woodcutter.

39

Time passes Hansel and Gretel grow stronger by the day. They become the family that you never knew you wanted. You're happy together.

TURN THE PAGE.

Yet late at night, the fear eats at you. You hear the sound in your sleep — *Thwack! Thwack! Thwack!* In your dreams the woodcutter comes for his children.

But his children are yours now. You won't let anyone take Hansel and Gretel from you. And you'll never let them leave.

THE END

TO FOLLOW ANOTHER PATH, TURN TO PAGE 9.

You've made your point. The children are terrified. Perhaps you've taken this too far. You step to the side, away from the open doorway.

"Go," you say. But the children won't budge. They're too scared.

You step toward them to shoo them out the door. Hansel must have thought you were going to harm them. He grabs your oil lamp and tosses it near your feet. The glass shatters everywhere. The children run out of the house as fast as their legs can carry them. You step out to watch them disappear into the woods.

41

They won't be coming back, you think. As you stare out into the woods, the smell of baking gingerbread fills your nostrils. No, not baking. *Burning!* The lamp!

TURN THE PAGE.

You whirl around. The spilled oil has spread all over the floor right to the edge of the oven. The oil has caught fire, along with your gingerbread walls!

You scream for help, but it's too late to stop it. The fire is spreading. From outside you watch helplessly as your precious home burns. The sight makes you weep. But the smell . . . the smell makes you *hungry*.

THE END

TO FOLLOW ANOTHER PATH, TURN TO PAGE 9.

Enough is enough. Now that you've gotten a better look at the frightened children, you feel guilty for trying to scare them. They look like they're half-starved.

"Come now, children," you say trying to soften your voice. They back away, one small step at a time. Gretel is getting awfully close to your hot oven.

"My oven is piping hot," you warn her. She stumbles, teetering toward the oven. You're terrified that she might fall inside and burn herself. As quickly as you can, you dash forward and grab the little girl's arm just before she goes down.

"No!" shouts Hansel. "You leave my sister alone!"

You can only imagine what this must look like to them. You're holding Gretel in front of the oven right after telling the children that you were going to eat them! What have you done?

"No, no, children," you try to explain. How can you gain their trust? A cake! Children love cake! If you bake them one, they'd be sure to trust you.

You look Hansel in the eyes. "I'll bake you—"

"No!" he interrupts. "She wants to bake us, Gretel!"

Together the children charge at you. They may be small, but their desperation has made them strong. They slam into you, throwing you off balance. You try to regain your footing, stumbling into your table and sending a pan of gingerbread crashing to the floor. Then Hansel charges again, throwing his body into yours.

This time you topple into the oven. Your final thought: *This is hot enough for gingerbread now.*

THE END

TO FOLLOW ANOTHER PATH, TURN TO PAGE 9.

44

CHAPTER 3

Hansel and Gretel in Space

"Hansel, we're getting too far out," you scold. The stars race by you as your brother pilots your ship through deep space.

"Nonsense," says Hansel. "Look, there's the Orion Nebula right over there. We're practically in our backyard."

You glance down at your instrument panel. "We're more than 20 light years from home. Dad said we couldn't go more than 10."

"Don't worry," Hansel says. "I know right where I'm at."

You scowl. Hansel would never admit to being lost, and you both know it.

"If you're so worried, we'll drop some beacons along the way so we don't get lost," Hansel says as he presses a button. A loud *Thunk!* rattles the ship as a beacon drops out of your tiny cargo bay. The beacon instantly shows up on your navigation screen as a blinking green dot.

Your little ship zooms through hyperspace. You buzz by a planet and sling past an asteroid. Every few minutes Hansel drops another beacon. Green dots blink happily on your screen.

"Whoa, check it out," Hansel says.

You look up from your panel as the ship drops out of hyperspace. There before you is a large brown and pink planet. A set of brilliant rings reflects light back at you.

"That's weird," you say checking your charts. "There's not supposed to be anything here."

"An uncharted planet!" Hansel says excitedly. "We gotta check this out. Prepare for atmospheric entry."

Your first instinct is to object. But the chance to step foot on a planet nobody has ever seen? That's too tempting to resist. You strap in as the ship descends.

"Here we go," Hansel calls out. "Landing in 5 . . . 4 . . . 3 . . . 2 . . . 1." *Clunk!* the ship touches down.

"Let's go check it out," Hansel says.

Within seconds you're bounding out of the hatch. The ground is dark brown. It cracks and squishes beneath your feet.

You carefully open the visor of your helmet. A familiar smell fills the air. Could it be? You snap off a piece of the ground and bring it to your lips. "Hansel, this planet is made of *chocolate*!"

Hansel bends over a bright pink bush. "And this is cotton candy!" he says. Hansel grabs a giant clump and stuffs it into his mouth. "A planet made of candy, all for us! Let's eat!"

As you stuff a handful of delicious, gooey chocolate into your mouth, the ground begins to shake. A giant *ROOOAAAAR!* booms through the air. You both freeze.

"Um," you whisper. "I don't think we're alone here, Hansel."

51

TO RUN FOR YOUR SHIP,
TURN TO PAGE 52.

TO INVESTIGATE THE NOISE,
TURN TO PAGE 54.

"Run!" you shout. You practically trip over each other in your hurry to get back to your ship. The ground shakes as you dive into your seats and strap in.

"Beginning takeoff routine," Hansel says.

"Skip the routine!" you yell. "Just punch it!"

Hansel reaches out his hand and whacks a bright red button. The rocket engines roar to life, burning fuel at maximum power. The ship rattles and surges, but it doesn't budge.

"What's wrong?" Hansel asks. "Why aren't we going?"

You look down at the ground. The chocolate under the ship has become a thick goo.

"The engines are melting the chocolate!" you shout. "We're stuck!"

"That's the least of our problems," Hansel says, pointing. "Look!"

Your ship is enveloped in an enormous shadow. It seems like a mountain has sprung up in front of your ship. But this is no mountain. It's a great green glowing glob of goo, and it's staring down at you!

The space glob opens its huge mouth and belches, "THIS IS MY CANDY!" Two arms pop out of the glob and extend down toward the ship.

TO TRY TO COMMUNICATE WITH THE SPACE GLOB, TURN TO PAGE 56.

TO OPEN FIRE, TURN TO PAGE 61.

As the echoes of the giant roar die down, Hansel looks at you. "We gotta check this out," he says.

"It came from that way," you reply, pointing toward what appears to be a volcano. The mountain rises straight up out of the ground and is topped by a wide crater.

You grab a hunk of chocolate and nibble away as the two of you trek toward the volcano. It's steep up the face of the mountain. But it's made of sticky toffee, which gives good traction for the climb.

As you near the top, you stop at a wide outcropping. Both of you crane your necks up to get a better look. That's when you spot it. Something is moving up there. From down here it's tough to tell just what it is. But it's big, green, and globby.

"It's an alien life form!" Hansel says. "We're gonna be famous!"

First contact with a new species of alien life would be huge news back home. You can just imagine all the attention you'd get — medals, parades, parties. But as you look up at the hulking beast on the mountaintop, you shudder. Is first contact really such a good idea?

TO APPROACH THE ALIEN,
TURN TO PAGE 57.

TO RUN BACK TO THE SHIP AND GET OFF THIS PLANET,
TURN TO PAGE 68.

55

You flip a switch to activate the ship's external loudspeaker.

"We're sorry!" you tell the glob. "We didn't know the candy belonged to you. We promise we won't eat another bite. It's all yours!"

The glob looms over the ship, as if deep in thought.

"I'll let you go," the glob begins, the boom of its bloblike voice rattling the entire ship, "but first you need to come out of that ship."

You flip off the speaker. "Don't do it!" Hansel warns you. "It's a trap!"

"Are we still stuck?" you ask. Hansel nods his head. You're running out of options.

TO EXIT THE SHIP,
TURN TO PAGE 64.

TO REFUSE TO LEAVE,
TURN TO PAGE 66.

"Let's meet this alien," you say confidently, grabbing hold of a sticky toffee outcropping and pulling yourself up.

The top of the mountain sinks down into a giant crater. You peer down inside to see roiling, bubbling brown lava.

"Well that seems about right," Hansel whispers. You both inhale a wonderful scent. "That isn't lava at all. That's caramel!"

In another time and place, a chocolate planet with a molten caramel core would be hard to overlook. But here and now, your eyes are fixed on the great green glob standing before you. The alien is perched over the edge of the crater. It appears to be lowering something down into the caramel.

TURN THE PAGE.

It's a giant pretzel! The alien sings to itself as it dips the pretzel — which has to be as big as you are — into the crater of bubbling caramel. You can just barely make out the tune.

"Dip them, dry them, roll them in nuts.

Bite them, eat them, crunch up their guts!"

Suddenly the glob turns around. "Oooh! Company!" it squeals. "Just in time for a snack! Come closer, my friends. My, my, don't you look delish . . . I mean delightful!"

Before you can say anything, Hansel walks toward the alien to introduce himself. You start to step forward. Something about this feels wrong though.

TO FOLLOW HANSEL AND TALK TO THE ALIEN, TURN TO PAGE 59.

TO TELL HANSEL TO RUN, TURN TO PAGE 70.

58

"Hansel!" you cry, but it's too late. He's already walking up to the alien. You have no choice but to follow him.

"Hello," he calls out. "We're Hansel and Gretel, from the planet Earth. We love your planet."

The glob's eyes light up at the compliment. "Oh, you do?" the glob says. "That's lovely. Tell me now, you didn't nibble on my planet, did you?"

"Of course not!" you lie and quickly wipe a smear of chocolate off of your face.

The glob quivers in a gesture that looks like **59** a nod. "Good, good. My, you are skinny little creatures," the glob says as it looks you over. "You really could use some fattening up. Come here. I'll prepare you with caramel. Errm, I mean I'll prepare you something to eat with caramel."

"Actually I think we need to get going now," you say. Hansel seems to be thinking the same thing, because he starts to back away from the drooling glob.

"Stop right there!" The glob's booming voice shakes the entire mountain. "Candy, candy, candy! All I ever get is candy. It's time for some meat!"

The glob moves with sudden and surprising speed, sliding along the edge of the crater toward you. But it may have moved a little too quickly. The glob seems to lose its balance. The great green mass quivers as it tries to get its footing.

60

TO CHARGE AT THE GLOB, TURN TO PAGE 72.

TO RUN, TURN TO PAGE 75.

The glob's green arms look tiny on its blobby body. But its hands are still twice the size of your whole ship. It plucks the ship out of the melted chocolate and lifts you toward its mouth.

Your ship isn't built for battle, but you've got some basic weapons. You take aim and fire your laser straight into the alien's open mouth.

"ARRRRRGH!" the alien screams.

The massive beast drops your ship like a toy. It slams back to the ground, bounces, and rolls straight into a lake of soda pop. Hansel desperately tries to start the engines, but it's useless. Bubbles fizz all around you as the ship begins to sink. You both bail out, diving into the soda and swimming for all you're worth.

"Yuck!" Hansel says, spitting. "It's lemon-lime! I *hate* lemon-lime soda!"

The two of you make it to the edge of the lake and duck into a cave made of toffee rocks. For the next several hours, you can hear the space glob outside searching for you. Every now and then, the glob burps causing the ground to shake.

In time the glob gives up. You and Hansel emerge from the cave. Your ship is lost. Nobody back home knows where you are. It's unlikely anyone will ever find your beacons.

"I guess this is home now," you say as you snap some bark off of a peanut brittle tree. You're already tired of sweets.

THE END

TO FOLLOW ANOTHER PATH, TURN TO PAGE 9.

"We have to leave the ship," you say to Hansel. "We can't go anywhere."

You take a deep breath and open the hatch. Carefully you step back down to the planet's surface. From outside the ship, the glob looks even bigger. You imagine that this must be what a mouse feels like looking up at you.

"Come closer," booms the glob.

With a hard gulp, you take a step. "What do you want?" Your voice cracks.

The glob leans in and sighs. "All this candy has rotted my teeth. I can't eat another bite. Could you take all this back to your home planet with you?"

You look around. You and Hansel can't possibly eat all this candy by yourselves. Then you get an idea.

"I've got a way to get rid of all this candy for you and pay for your dental work at the same time," you say.

You tell the glob your plan and shake hands. It even helps you load boulder-sized hunks of chocolate onto your ship. As the glob pulls your ship free, you say goodbye.

"We'll come back for more candy," you promise. The glob quivers with delight. You wave to your new business partner and fire up the rockets.

When you get back to Earth, you and Hansel set up a candy shop with your endless supply of candy.

You tell your customers, "These sweets are out of this world!"

THE END

TO FOLLOW ANOTHER PATH, TURN TO PAGE 9.

Hansel's right. This has to be a trap.

"No deal!" you announce over the speaker. "We're not stepping one foot out of this ship!"

The glob roars with anger. The entire ship shakes. The roaring grows louder and louder. You cover your ears but can't block out the sound.

The rattle in the ship grows more intense, until you hear a sharp *Crack!* Hansel gasps as the window splits in two. The sound of shattering glass briefly drowns out the roar of the glob.

That's when the alien grabs hold of your ship. Hansel scrambles to fire a laser beam at the raging alien, but it's too late. The glob picks up your ship.

"Stay away from my candy!" roars the glob as it throws you and your ship into a pit of boiling sugar syrup.

THE END

TO FOLLOW ANOTHER PATH, TURN TO PAGE 9.

"Um, Hansel," you say with a gulp.

"What?" he asks.

"I'm not sure I'm ready to say hello to that giant space glob up there," you say.

"Maybe you're right," Hansel says. "It might not be friendly."

Quietly the two of you sneak back down the mountainside. All the way down, you keep a wary eye at the top. The creature up there appears to be baking something. When the wind turns just right, you can smell the scent of caramel.

68

Back at the ship, you waste little time. Hansel uses the anti-gravity engines to slowly lift off the surface, then he punches the rocket engines. You roar back into space with a sigh of relief.

"Whew! We dodged that bullet," Hansel says.

You check the ship's readings. It's moving a bit slower than normal. "Hmm, I wonder what that extra drag is from on our ship," you murmur.

"Let's check when we get home," Hansel says. "I've had enough of deep space and alien blobs to last me a lifetime!"

THE END

TO FOLLOW ANOTHER PATH, TURN TO PAGE 9.

"Hansel, no!" you shout as you back away. But as always Hansel ignores you. He walks right up to the alien and extends his hand.

"I'm Hansel. Greetings from Planet Earth!" he says.

"Caramel-covered Earthlings!" the glob squeals, scooping up Hansel. "What a treat!"

Before you can try to stop it, the glob dips Hansel into the caramel and gobbles him up. Then the glob reaches for you. You turn to run but stumble and fall down the face of the mountain. You tumble down the sticky toffee rocks, all the way to the bottom. Luckily you land in a huge thicket of marshmallow bushes. You scramble to your feet. Above you the great green glob is in hot pursuit.

"Come back, my little morsel!" it bellows. "I want more!"

You run as fast as your feet will take you, climb into your ship, and take off. You're dreading going home. You're going to be in so much trouble for letting your brother become snack food. You wish you had never landed on this candy-coated planet.

THE END

TO FOLLOW ANOTHER PATH, TURN TO PAGE 9.

This could be your only chance. Running at full speed, you launch yourself into the air and slam into the giant glob's body. It feels like crashing into a giant water balloon.

At first it looks like your charge was a waste. The glob doesn't budge. But then the alien's body ripples from the impact. The wave rushes upward, throwing it off balance. The alien teeters on the edge of the crater, barely hanging on. At that moment Hansel comes flying at it. Your brother launches into the creature, and it finally topples over the edge. The glob roars as it plunges into the molten caramel lava. With a massive *Plop!*, it's gone.

"Now that," Hansel says staring down at the rippling molten caramel, "is a delicious way to go."

"Let's go home," you reply. Hansel just nods.

72

And so it's back to your ship. Before you take off, you load the cargo bay with all the candy you can carry.

"Maybe we shouldn't tell anyone about this place after all," Hansel suggests as the ship rises above the atmosphere.

You smile. "I'm with you." After all, what kid wouldn't want to keep a planet made entirely of candy for herself?

THE END

TO FOLLOW ANOTHER PATH, TURN TO PAGE 9.

"Hansel, run!" you shout as you turn and start to dash away. But the glob quickly finds its balance and catches you by your collar. It slides across the outer edge of the crater and scoops up Hansel in its other arm. You wriggle and struggle, but the alien holds you tight.

"No, no, no," it whispers with a sneer. It looks you up and down. "I think I'll roll you in nougat and nuts then drizzle you in butterscotch. Your brother should taste quite nice in a blueberry-and-human pie. What a lucky day!"

You couldn't disagree more.

THE END

TO FOLLOW ANOTHER PATH, TURN TO PAGE 9.

CHAPTER 4

Game Over

"Whoa, look at that!" you gasp as your friend Greta shows you her latest treasure.

"It's a VR-9000," she says proudly as she reaches behind her wheelchair and lifts a large headset out of a brightly colored box. "It's a state-of-the-art virtual reality gaming system."

"No way! Those things aren't even out yet!" you say.

Everyone has heard about the VR-9000. It's the first gaming system that plugs directly into a player's brain. By plugging into a data port at the base of the skull, it provides the most realistic virtual reality experience ever created.

77

"I read that these things had too many bugs to be released," you say. "The news said that the virtual reality is a bit *too* real."

"You know my dad," Greta says with a grin. "He's got connections. But that's not even the best news." Greta turns her wheelchair, reaches behind her desk, and pulls out a second box. She has two! "Wanna play?" she asks.

"Oh man, I sure do!" you answer, almost tripping over your own feet to get your hands on the system.

"There aren't any public virtual reality worlds to explore yet," Greta explains. "But I found a link to a game on the manufacturer's private server. A couple of quick hacks, and I was in. It's called *Unstable Build*. Nobody bothered to password-protect it, so we're good to go. Ready?"

You can't wipe the grin off your face. You nod your head and wait as Greta presses the START button.

In an instant Greta's room disappears. In its place stands a dark forest. A flickering blue oval glows behind you. It's a portal back to the real world — all you have to do is step through it, and the game will save your progress.

A cool breeze blows across your face. Birds chirp in the trees. A musty odor fills the air. It's all so real that you almost stumble. You look at Greta and see the biggest shock of them all. She looks the same, but . . . she's standing up! There's no wheelchair in sight.

"Amazing," you whisper.

"So this is what the view looks like from up here," Greta says with a smirk.

Greta has been paralyzed from the waist down since she was born. You can't imagine how strange this must feel to her. You realize that this experience is far more than a game for her. It's giving her a chance to experience the world in a whole new way.

You reach out to touch a tree. It's covered in soft, furry moss. The moss stains your hand green. You try to wipe it off, but your hand remains bright green.

"It must be one of those bugs people talked about," you suggest, still wiping your hand on your pants.

Just then a loud noise rings through your head. *Beep! Beep! Beep!* The sound seems to come from every direction.

"Whoa, what was that?" you ask.

"The system is telling us that my phone is ringing back in the real world," Greta says. "Darn, we just got here. What should we do?"

TO EXIT THE GAME, AND ANSWER THE PHONE, TURN TO PAGE 82.

TO IGNORE THE PHONE CALL, TURN TO PAGE 85.

The phone keeps ringing. "Grr! OK, you'd better see who's calling," you say.

Greta steps through the portal. Her avatar dissolves away, leaving you alone for a moment. With a deep breath, you step through. And just like that, you're back in Greta's room.

"Come on, Dad. How bad could it be?" Greta is already talking on the phone. "I mean it was super easy to exit out of the game." She talks for a few more minutes before she hangs up.

"Dad told one of his coworkers that he gave me a gaming system," she says to you. "Now he's worried that it's too dangerous for us to play. He said some nonsense about blurring the lines between the real and the virtual worlds."

You roll your eyes. Adults are always worrying about something.

You reach out to adjust your headset when you notice something that stops you cold.

"Whoa, what the heck?" You hold your hand out to Greta. It's stained green.

"No way!" she gasps. "How is that possible?"

You shake your head. "No clue. Maybe it's some advanced feature?"

You're a little spooked, but you both agree to go back into the game. Within seconds you find yourselves back in the dark forest. Greta is back on her feet. She skips and jumps through the woods, enjoying the use of her legs. You can barely keep up!

83

You continue through the woods until you seem a warm glow ahead. It's a house made entirely of candy!

Greta runs right up to the house and snaps off
a piece of a candy-cane fence. "Come on," she calls.

84   You stand there, your mind racing. You can
see how happy this game makes your friend. But
the green on your hand, the warning from Greta's
father — you can't get them out of your mind.

TO JOIN GRETA,
TURN TO PAGE 88.

TO LEAVE THE GAME,
TURN TO PAGE 94.

"Whoever it is can leave a voicemail," you say with a grin. "Let's explore!" The forest is vast. "How can we find our way back? If we get lost, the portal is worthless to us."

"Not a problem," Greta explains. "To leave just call out the words, 'exit simulation.' We'll lose our progress in the game if we leave that way, but it will get us out instantly."

Greta reaches into her pocket and pulls out a loaf of virtual bread. It smells like it's fresh out of the oven. "But we won't need to do that. I've got a plan," Greta says. As you and Greta walk, she tosses small bread crumbs onto the ground. "We'll just follow the crumbs back to the portal."

85

Greta skips ahead. You follow her along a trail through the woods. It winds through a deep gully and skirts along a lake with black water.

Strange animals scurry, imaginary insects buzz in your ear. You even spot some troll tracks.

"This place is great," you say.

"And it just got better," Greta says. "Look!"

A house stands before you. But it's not like any house you've ever seen. It's made entirely of sweets — from the gingerbread walls to the candy-cane fence.

"Hey, you kids," a voice rings out, startling you. Someone is coming toward you. It's an old woman shuffling along with what appears to be a broom handle. "What are you two doing out here alone? Come inside, let's have something to eat."

"I'm not sure we should," Greta whispers, slowly backing away. "If I know my fairy tales, that is an evil witch. Of course if it's only a simulation . . ."

"Now, now," the old woman croaks. "I get lonely here in the forest all by myself. Come have some tea with me!"

TO GO INSIDE THE WOMAN'S HOUSE, TURN TO PAGE 93.

TO REFUSE, TURN TO 100.

A house made of gingerbread in a virtual world — who wouldn't want a taste? You reach up and snap off a section of the house. As you bite into it, your mouth is filled with the rich flavor of gingerbread. It's sweet and melts in your mouth.

"Ooh," says Greta. "This is the tastiest thing I've ever eaten."

"And it's not even real," you say taking another bite. "We could eat this all day and never get a bellyache!"

Greta breaks off another huge hunk, splits it in half, and hands you a piece. The two of you "ooh" and "ahh" as you munch away. When the door to the house swings open, you jump so hard that you almost choke.

"Nibble, nibble," calls a voice from inside. A figure emerges in the doorway. It's an old woman. Her back is bent and crooked. Her face is lined with wrinkles. But her eyes glow a brilliant emerald. They look you up and down in a way that makes you shiver.

Your heart is racing. But Greta seems to be having a grand time. "Whoa! Are you a witch?" she squeals with glee.

In a flash the crooked old woman darts out of the door. She seems to double in size, taking on a towering, menacing appearance. Before either of you can react, she grabs Greta by the shirt and lifts her off the ground.

89

TO RUSH TO GRETA'S AID,
TURN TO PAGE 90.

TO EXIT THE SIMULATION,
TURN TO PAGE 92.

"Let her go!" you shout, charging.

With the flick of a wrist, the witch sends you flying backward through the air. You slam up against a large tree trunk. Your body aches. You can barely breathe. As you try to stand, pain shoots through you. It feels like your ribs are broken. What kind of simulation is this?

The witch drags you both inside her house. Still doubled over in pain, you watch as she ties Greta to a chair next to you. From floor to ceiling, the room is adorned in sweets. Candy canes, gum drops, cupcakes — it'd be a kid's dream, if not for the witch. She throws you on a bed in a corner as she stokes a fire in a large brick oven.

"What do we do?" you whisper to Greta.

"I know this story," Greta answers. "I think we're supposed to shove the witch into the oven."

You breathe in short, shallow huffs. The pain is growing worse by the moment. You're not sure you want anything more to do with this game.

TO EXIT THE SIMULATION AND BE DONE WITH THIS GAME,
TURN TO PAGE 92.

TO TRY TO PUSH THE WITCH INTO THE OVEN,
TURN TO PAGE 104.

"Exit simulation!" you command.

One moment you're standing there in the game. The next everything melts away, and you're back in Greta's room. Your friend is there next to you. She's as motionless as a stone. For some reason she hasn't exited the simulation yet.

Minutes pass. What is she doing in there? Why hasn't she followed you out? Greta's body begins to tremble. She whimpers and groans as if she's in pain. Suddenly she lets loose a blood-curdling scream.

TO SHUT DOWN THE SYSTEM,
TURN TO PAGE 96.

TO RE-ENTER THE SIMULATION,
TURN TO PAGE 98.

You look at Greta and shrug your shoulders. You'd never go into a stranger's house in real life, but this isn't real life.

"I've got cookies in the oven," the woman croaks as she leads you through her front door. The house smells just like a bakery. "I'll get us some cookies and milk so we can chat," she says.

"Are you a witch?" Greta blurts out.

The woman turns slowly. A darkness comes over her eyes. "Why yes, I am," she says coldly, thrusting a plate of cookies onto the table. "Now eat!"

The two of you can only stare as the woman turns back to get another sheet of cookies out of the oven. One thing is certain. There's no way you're eating those cookies now.

93

TO EXIT THE GAME, TURN TO PAGE 95.

TO ATTACK THE WITCH, TURN TO PAGE 102.

"Greta, this is a bad idea. I think—" Before you can even get the sentence out, the door to the house bursts open. An old woman rushes out, swatting at you with a broomstick.

"Run!" you shout.

Greta, with a large hunk of gingerbread still in her hand, doesn't hesitate. Together you bound through the forest. Finally, huffing for breath, you both collapse onto the grass in a small meadow that overlooks a crystal clear pond.

"That was *crazy!*" Greta gasps. "Running is awesome!"

You start to laugh. The fun is cut short when you hear a distant voice. "Come back here, you little thieves!"

GO TO PAGE 95.

"Enough is enough," Greta says. "Let's get back to the real world. Exit simulation!"

Greta disappears before your very eyes. You shake your head. This game is too much for you.

"Exit simulation," you command. And in an instant, you're back in Greta's room.

"Shut that thing down," you tell your friend. "I'm in no mood for adventure right now."

"Yeah, me neither," Greta agrees, turning off the system. "Let's go out into the *real* world instead."

THE END

95

TO FOLLOW ANOTHER PATH, TURN TO PAGE 9.

Your heart is racing. What's happening to your friend? You have to stop the game. You rush to the wall and yank the system's plug out of the outlet.

The low hum of the computer's cooling fans winds down. You unplug the headset from your friend's data port and lift the unit from her head. Greta's face is locked in an expression of pure terror.

"Greta!" you call. You tap her shoulder. You shake her. Nothing you do wakes her. It's as if she is still in the machine even though you unplugged it.

"No!" you scream. You reboot the system and try running the simulation again. Every time you do, you just get an error message. No matter what you try, the game will not open.

You frantically call 9-1-1 for help. The ambulance arrives within minutes. At the hospital the doctors have no idea what the problem is.

"There doesn't seem to be anything physically wrong with her," the doctors explain to Greta's parents. "Her brainwaves *look* like she's awake and very active. In fact they look a lot like the brainwaves of someone having a nightmare."

Weeks, months, years pass. Your friend never returns. Her body remains, but her mind is lost. You dream about the game almost every night. In them Greta is locked inside a gingerbread house, calling for you. The dream always ends the same way — with you calling out, "Exit simulation!"

THE END

TO FOLLOW ANOTHER PATH, TURN TO PAGE 9.

What's going on? Why isn't she exiting? You can't wait any longer. You quickly plug yourself in and jump back into the simulation. The virtual world springs up around you.

You're greeted by a wicked cackling. The witch stands over you, grinning a big toothless grin. Tied up behind her, you see your friend. Greta's mouth is covered with a band of cloth.

"Ooh, such a lucky day!" the witch howls gleefully.

"Let her go!" you demand. You remind yourself that this isn't real. You can leave any time you wish. Yet you're still terrified.

"And why would I do such a thing?" the witch barks back. "Here I am, all alone in this terrible world. And along you come, eating *my* house. Then you get to just disappear."

"And I'll do it again," you say boldly. "And I'm taking Greta with me!"

The witch leans in closer. Her breath smells of death and decay. "No, young one. You won't be leaving this time."

Before you can exit again, the witch grabs you and shoves a piece of cloth into your mouth. She holds you tight as she ties your wrists and ankles together.

"Eggggsit Shimulashun," you say through the gag.

But you can't get the words out. The program doesn't recognize the command. You're trapped!

The witch cackles. "Foolish child. You never should have come back. Now you're mine forever!"

THE END

TO FOLLOW ANOTHER PATH, TURN TO PAGE 9.

Something about the invitation just doesn't feel right.

"I don't think so," you say, backing away.

"Please, oh please!" begs the old woman, slowly stepping closer. "I can't say how long it's been since I had visitors. It's a cold and lonely world inside this machine. Stay for a bit."

You get chills. Did she say *inside this machine?* She couldn't possibly know that, could she?

The look on Greta's face tells you that she heard it too. She grabs you by the arm. "Let's go!"

You return to your bread-crumb trail. Only something is different. The bread crumbs are gone — replaced by deep footprints. You follow them to the portal, expecting to find the old woman waiting for you there. But to your relief, she's nowhere to be seen.

You go through the portal first, followed by Greta. For a moment you're blinded by the bright lights in the room. As your eyes adjust, however, your blood runs cold.

"Welcome back," says the old woman, standing by the edge of Greta's bed. Somehow, some way, she has stepped through the portal into the real world! Greta faints in her wheelchair. You feel your own knees growing weak.

The woman no longer seems old and frail. Now she stands tall and straight. An aura of magic and power surrounds her. She raises an arm and begins to chant unfamiliar words. You barely have time to scream before a column of flames engulfs you.

THE END

TO FOLLOW ANOTHER PATH, TURN TO PAGE 9.

The plate of cookies sits in front of you. Greta seems frozen in fear. That means that it's up to you.

The witch turns her back to tend to her oven. With one motion you sweep the plate of cookies to the floor. *Crash!* The plate shatters into a thousand tiny pieces.

Before the sound of the crash fades away, you take off. The witch whirls around, just as you launch yourself toward her. Your shoulder slams into her chest. The impact sends her toppling backward and straight into the oven. She opens her mouth and lets out a terrible scream. It seems to fill the entire house, the entire world.

The flames engulf her. The scream grows louder and louder. You throw your hands over your ears, but it doesn't help. The world around you starts to flicker.

Instead of gingerbread walls, you see panels of ones and zeros. The scream changes into something that sounds like static.

Then in an instant, it's gone — the house, the forest, everything. All that remains in an endless virtual nothing is you and Greta. Your friend stares at you with her mouth hanging open.

With one last look at the vast emptiness, you stand and call out, "Exit simulation." But you already have. You just can't get back to the real world. You're trapped somewhere in between.

THE END
TO FOLLOW ANOTHER PATH, TURN TO PAGE 9.

Do you have to defeat the witch to win the game? Your lungs burn. You groan as you try to stand. The floor creaks beneath your feet.

"You're in no condition to get up," says the witch without turning around.

It's now or never. You ignore the pain and dart across the room. You slam into the witch with all your might. She screams as she falls forward into the fire. It's a blood-curdling sound that seems to shake the entire virtual world. The house around you flickers and starts to break into pixels.

"The program is crashing!" Greta shouts. "Exit simulation!" You watch as your friend disappears.

"Exit simulation!" you cry. In the last moment before the virtual world melts away, you catch a glimpse of a figure emerging from the oven.

Then it's gone. Only Greta's room remains. You collapse onto Greta's bed.

That should be that. After all it was just a game, right? But back in the real world, your lungs still ache. You look over at Greta, and you can't believe your eyes. She's still standing. She can walk!

Later you are both taken to the hospital. There you're treated for three broken ribs. The doctors say Greta's recovery is a miracle.

"What happened?" the doctor asks you as he examines your green hand. You don't even know where to begin.

THE END

TO FOLLOW ANOTHER PATH, TURN TO PAGE 9.

CHAPTER 5

THE TALE
OF THE TALE

For hundreds of years, the story of Hansel and Gretel has delighted and terrified children. The tale's origin has been lost to history.

Today historians can only guess about its true beginnings. One theory is that the story started during a period called the Great Famine (1315–1317). This food shortage struck Europe, leaving millions of people starving. During this time many parents were forced to make a terrible decision — starve together or abandon their children. The story of Hansel and Gretel, who were abandoned in the woods, could have sprung from this dark period.

Another theory is that the tale may have grown out of a popular type of story from the 1600s and 1700s. In these stories children escaped from ogres that had captured them. The ogre may have evolved into a witch, with the rest of the story growing around that idea.

By the 1800s several versions of the tale existed. In some Hansel and Gretel were cast out by their stepmother. In others it was their biological mother. The details varied, but the basic plot was the same. In 1812 brothers Jacob and Wilhelm Grimm published a version

of this story in their collection, *Kinder- und Hausmärchen*. Today this volume is called *Grimms' Fairy Tales*. The Brothers Grimm titled their story "Hansel and Gretel," and the name stuck.

The story grew in popularity when composer Engelbert Humperdinck adapted it for the opera. His "Hänsel und Gretel" opera opened on December 23, 1893. It quickly became a Christmas tradition and is still performed today.

This story is hundreds of years old. Yet we still find references to it in modern language. One of the most iconic aspects of Hansel and Gretel is the trail of bread crumbs the children leave to find their way back home. Today the phrase "trail of bread crumbs" means to use any string of clues or evidence to find a location or reach a conclusion.

Hansel and Gretel is a timeless tale that continues to make an impact. The way we live, act, and think has changed a lot over the centuries. But the tale of two children, lost and afraid, stands the test of time.

OTHER PATHS TO EXPLORE

1. Hansel and Gretel met the witch after stumbling on her candy house. Imagine you were building a house that you could eat. What foods would you use? Why?

2. In chapter 3 we hear the fairy tale from the witch's perspective. Reading a story from another character's point of view can change the way you see events. Think of another fairy tale. How does the story change when you put yourself in the villain's shoes?

3. Think of your own version of "Hansel and Gretel." What kind of setting would you use? Would it be a classic retelling of the fairy tale, or would you give it a modern spin? How would your setting impact the actions of Hansel, Gretel, and the witch?

READ MORE

Gunderson, Jessica. *Cinderella: An Interactive Fairy Tale Adventure.* You Choose: Fractured Fairy Tales. North Mankato, Minn.: Capstone Press, 2016.

Harper, Benjamin. *Hansel & Gretel & Zombies: A Graphic Novel.* Far Out Fairy Tales. North Mankato, Minn.: Stone Arch Books, 2016.

Schwartz, Corey Rosen, and Rebecca J. Gomez. *Hensel and Gretel, Ninja Chicks.* New York: G.P. Putnam's Sons, 2016.

INTERNET SITES

Use FactHound to find Internet sites related to this book.

Visit *www.facthound.com*

Just type in 9781515769446 and go.

LOOK FOR ALL THE BOOKS IN THIS SERIES:

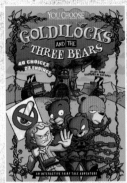